Ants at Work

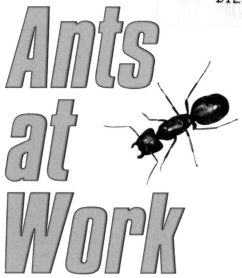

Written by David Neufeld

Celebration Press

Parsippany, New Jersey

If you were an ant, you'd probably spend your whole life working with your mother and your sisters.

Ants live together in a colony.
A colony starts with a queen.

The queen ant finds a comfortable nest. Her nest might be under a rock, in a wall, or under the ground. There she lays her first eggs.

The queen lays about an egg a day. After a few days the eggs turn into larvae. Larvae are young, wormlike forms of insects.

The queen ant feeds and takes care of the larvae. They are helpless and cannot move.

After a couple of weeks, many larvae spin cocoons. Ants at this stage are called pupae. The pupae do not eat or move for another three weeks.

Soon the pupae emerge from their cocoons. They look like other ants. They are smaller but can take care of themselves. These young ants will be the queen's first workers.

When the young ants have grown stronger, they start to work. Then the queen spends all her time laying more eggs.

The queen now has a small colony. The young ants start digging, hunting, or cleaning. They are all workers and they are all females.

Digging ants keep adding on to the nest until there are about a hundred rooms— enough space for many workers.

Some colonies have as few as 12 ants. Other colonies might have as many as 1 million ants!

Hunting ants look for food. They leave a trail of scent everywhere they walk. If many ants use the same trail, the scent gets very strong. That tells the ants that it's an important path.

When an ant finds food, she taps
other ants to show it to them.
Soon there is an ant superhighway
leading from the nest to the
food and back again.

Ants can lift things that are much heavier than they are. If an ant were as big as a person, it could lift a car right off the ground.

This strength helps the ant carry a lot of food back to the nest.

The cleaning ants stay behind in the nest.
They feed the queen and the baby ants.
Then they clean up after everybody.

All of the eggs that the queen lays at first are workers. But after the colony has grown to a larger size, new queens begin to hatch.

These new queens cannot stay in the colony. Unlike workers, they grow wings. They will use their wings to fly away to start new colonies. There can only be one queen in a colony.

Ants work their whole lives. If you were an ant, which kind of ant would you want to be?